CHINESE IDIOM STORIES

成语故事

PART 63

ANAN MA

马安安

ACKNOWLEDGEMENT

Chinese idioms have a history of thousands of years. There are thousands of Chinese idioms. In this book, I have selected some of the must-know Chinese idioms. In particular, these idioms are very important for the students for the Chinese culture and language enthusiasts. I feel excited to share the knowledge of Chinese language and culture with the students of Mandarin Chinese. I wish to take this opportunity to thank everyone who helped me complete this book.

ANAN MA

INTRODUCTION

Welcome to Chinese Idiom Stories series. In this series of books, you will learn Chinese idiom stories. Each book contains about 20 well-known Chinese idioms and the corresponding idiom stories. For each of the idioms, its English interpretation, pinyin, idiom story in Chinese as well as in English has been included. The keywords for the Chinese stories have been included for the readers to understand the Chinese versions of the stories better. In particular, the books are designed for the foreign students of Mandarin Chinese to improve their Chinese reading skills. Together, the series contains hundreds of must-know Chinese idiom stories. The books are suitable for all HSK level students.

CONTENTS

ACKNOWLEDGEMENT 2

INTRODUCTION 3

CONTENTS 4

Chapter 1: 刚柔并济 9

   1）成语名称 9

   2）成语的拼音 9

   3）英文意思 9

   4）成语故事（新编） 9

   5）关键词拼音 9

   6）英文故事 10

Chapter 2: 迎头赶上 11

   1）成语名称 11

   2）成语的拼音 11

   3）英文意思 11

   4）成语故事（新编） 11

   5）关键词拼音 11

   6）英文故事 12

Chapter 3: 自立为王 13

   1）成语名称 13

   2）成语的拼音 13

   3）英文意思 13

   4）成语故事（新编） 13

   5）关键词拼音 13

   6）英文故事 14

Chapter 4: 枉杀无辜 15

   1）成语名称 15

   2）成语的拼音 15

3）英文意思 15

4）成语故事（新编） 15

5）关键词拼音 15

6）英文故事 16

Chapter 5: 金钱非万能 18

1）成语名称 18

2）成语的拼音 18

3）英文意思 18

4）成语故事（新编） 18

5）关键词拼音 18

6）英文故事 19

Chapter 6: 登高远眺 20

1）成语名称 20

2）成语的拼音 20

3）英文意思 20

4）成语故事（新编） 20

5）关键词拼音 20

6）英文故事 21

Chapter 7: 养生送死 22

1）成语名称 22

2）成语的拼音 22

3）英文意思 22

4）成语故事（新编） 22

5）关键词拼音 22

6）英文故事 23

Chapter 8: 意味深长 24

1. 成语名称 24

2. 成语的拼音 24

3. 英文意思 24

4. 成语故事（新编） 24

5. 故事中关键词的拼音 24

6. 英文故事 24

Chapter 9: 不声不响 26

1. 成语名称 26

2. 成语的拼音 26

3. 英文意思 26

4. 成语故事（新编） 26

5. 故事中关键词的拼音 26

6. 英文故事 26

Chapter 10: 多一事不如少一事 28

1. 成语名称 28

2. 成语的拼音 28

3. 英文意思 28

4. 成语故事（新编） 28

5. 故事中关键词的拼音 28

6. 英文故事 28

Chapter 11: 一步到位 30

1. 成语名称 30

2. 成语的拼音 30

3. 英文意思 30

4. 成语故事（新编） 30

5. 故事中关键词的拼音 30

6. 英文故事 30

Chapter 12: 待人诚恳 32

1. 成语名称 32

2. 成语的拼音 32

3. 英文意思 32

4. 成语故事（新编） 32

5. 故事中关键词的拼音 32

6. 英文故事 32

Chapter 13: 同性相斥 34

1）成语名称 34

2）成语的拼音 34

3）英文意思 34

4）成语故事（新编） 34

5）关键词拼音 34

6）英文故事 35

Chapter 14: 咄咄逼人 36

1）成语名称 36

2）成语的拼音 36

3）英文意思 36

4）成语故事（新编） 36

5）关键词拼音 36

6）英文故事 37

Chapter 15: 树欲静而风不止 38

1）成语名称 38

2）成语的拼音 38

3）英文意思 38

4）成语故事（新编） 38

5）关键词拼音 38

6）英文故事 39

Chapter 16: 火中取栗 40

1）成语名称 40

2）成语的拼音 40

3）英文意思 40

4）成语故事（新编） 40

5）关键词拼音 40

6）英文故事 41

Chapter 17: 功夫不负有心人 42

    1）成语名称 42

    2）成语的拼音 42

    3）英文意思 42

    4）成语故事（新编） 42

    5）关键词拼音 42

    6）英文故事 43

Chapter 18: 载歌载舞 44

    1）成语名称 44

    2）成语的拼音 44

    3）英文意思 44

    4）成语故事（新编） 44

    5）关键词拼音 44

    6）英文故事 45

Chapter 19: 排忧解难 46

    1）成语名称 46

    2）成语的拼音 46

    3）英文意思 46

    4）成语故事（新编） 46

    5）关键词拼音 46

    6）英文故事 47

Chapter 20: 摩肩接踵 48

    1）成语名称 48

    2）成语的拼音 48

    3）英文意思 48

    4）成语故事（新编） 48

    5）关键词拼音 48

    6）英文故事 49

Chapter 1: 刚柔并济

1）成语名称

刚柔并济

2）成语的拼音

gāng róu bìng jì

3）英文意思

To combine firmness with flexibility; to balance rigor and leniency.

4）成语故事（新编）

在古代，有一位名叫李将军的将领，他以其卓越的军事才能和独特的领导风格闻名遐迩。李将军在治军上，既严格又慈爱，展现出了刚柔并济的智慧。

在一次战役前夕，李将军对士兵们进行了严格的训练，要求他们纪律严明，武艺精湛，不容丝毫懈怠。他的严格让士兵们心生敬畏，训练效果显著提升。然而，在训练之余，李将军又常常与士兵们促膝长谈，关心他们的生活疾苦，倾听他们的心声。他的慈爱让士兵们感受到了家的温暖，更加坚定了跟随他征战的决心。

战役打响后，李将军的军队如同猛虎下山，势不可挡。士兵们既勇猛无畏，又灵活多变，能够迅速适应战场形势的变化，最终取得了辉煌的胜利。人们都说，这多亏了李将军刚柔并济的治军之道。

5）关键词拼音

- 李将军：Lǐ jiāng jūn
- 军事才能：jūn shì cái néng
- 独特：dú tè
- 严格：yán gé
- 慈爱：cí ài
- 敬畏：jìng wèi
- 促膝长谈：cù xī cháng tán

- 勇猛无畏：yǒng měng wú wèi
- 灵活多变：líng huó duō biàn
- 辉煌：huī huáng

6）英文故事

In ancient times, there was a renowned general named Li, known for his exceptional military prowess and a unique leadership style that embodied the principle of combining firmness with flexibility.

Prior to a crucial battle, General Li subjected his soldiers to rigorous training, demanding impeccable discipline and mastery of martial arts, allowing no room for slackness. His strictness inspired awe among the troops, and their training results soared. Yet, amidst the intensity, General Li often engaged in heartfelt conversations with his soldiers, inquiring about their personal struggles and listening to their concerns. His kindness made the soldiers feel a sense of belonging, further strengthening their resolve to follow him into battle.

When the battle commenced, General Li's army descended upon the enemy like a fierce tiger, unstoppable. The soldiers fought with bravery, unafraid, and adapted swiftly to the shifting dynamics of the battlefield, ultimately securing a triumphant victory. People attributed this success to General Li's governance philosophy of balancing rigor and leniency, a true manifestation of the harmony between strength and gentleness.

Chapter 2: 迎头赶上

1）成语名称

迎头赶上

2）成语的拼音

yíng tóu gǎn shàng

3）英文意思

To catch up swiftly by confronting and overcoming obstacles head-on.

4）成语故事（新编）

在一个偏远的小山村里，住着一个小男孩叫小明。小明家境贫寒，但他聪明好学，对知识的渴望如同山间清泉，永不干涸。然而，由于条件限制，他比城里的孩子晚了好几年才开始接触书本。

每当看到同龄人已经能够流利地读书写字时，小明心里既羡慕又着急。但他没有放弃，而是决定迎头赶上。每天清晨，当第一缕阳光穿透山林，小明便开始了他的学习之旅。他利用一切可以利用的资源，无论是借来的旧课本，还是村里老先生偶尔的指点，都如饥似渴地吸收着。

日复一日，年复一年，小明凭借着不懈的努力和坚定的信念，逐渐缩小了与同龄人的差距。他的成绩突飞猛进，甚至在学校的比赛中获得了优异成绩，让所有人都刮目相看。小明用自己的行动诠释了"迎头赶上"的真谛，证明了只要勇于面对挑战，不断努力，就能后来居上。

5）关键词拼音

- 小明：Xiǎo Míng
- 山村：shān cūn
- 贫寒：pín hán
- 渴望：kě wàng
- 条件限制：tiáo jiàn xiàn zhì
- 流利：liú lì

- 着急：zháo jí
- 迎头赶上：yíng tóu gǎn shàng
- 不懈努力：bù xiè nǔ lì
- 坚定信念：jiān dìng xìn niàn
- 突飞猛进：tū fēi měng jìn
- 刮目相看：guā mù xiāng kàn

6）英文故事

In a remote mountain village lived a young boy named Xiao Ming. Born into poverty, Xiao Ming was nonetheless intelligent and eager for knowledge, his thirst for learning akin to an ever-flowing spring in the mountains. However, due to limited resources, he was several years behind his urban peers in accessing books.

Witnessing his friends already proficient in reading and writing, Xiao Ming felt both envy and urgency. Yet, he refused to be deterred, choosing instead to confront and overcome these obstacles head-on. Every dawn, as the first rays of sunshine pierced through the forest, Xiao Ming embarked on his journey of learning. He utilized every available resource, from borrowed, worn textbooks to occasional guidance from the village's elderly scholar, absorbing knowledge voraciously.

Days turned into years, and with unwavering effort and steadfast belief, Xiao Ming gradually narrowed the gap with his peers. His academic performance soared, even earning him accolades in school competitions that left everyone in awe. Xiao Ming's story embodied the essence of "catching up swiftly by confronting and overcoming obstacles head-on," proving that with courage, perseverance, and a resolute heart, one can indeed surpass expectations and achieve greatness.

Chapter 3: 自立为王

1）成语名称

自立为王

2）成语的拼音

zì lì wéi wáng

3）英文意思

To establish oneself as a king or leader, symbolizing independence and self-governance.

4）成语故事（新编）

在古代，有一个偏远的小国，名叫云隐国。云隐国地处群山环抱之中，资源匮乏，常受邻近大国的欺凌。国王年迈体弱，无力治理国家，国内民不聊生，百姓们生活在水深火热之中。

在这样一个时代背景下，云隐国中有一位年轻的勇士，名叫李昂。他英勇善战，智慧过人，更重要的是，他心怀大志，梦想着能让云隐国摆脱困境，自立为王，成为自己命运的主宰。

李昂深知，仅凭一己之力难以实现这一宏愿，于是他开始团结国内有志之士，共同商讨对策。他们加强军事训练，提升国力；同时，李昂还亲自出使邻国，以智慧和勇气赢得了邻国的尊重，为云隐国争取到了宝贵的和平发展时间。

经过多年的努力，云隐国在李昂的带领下逐渐强盛起来。最终，在一次盛大的庆典上，李昂正式宣布云隐国自立为王，成为了一个独立自主的国家。百姓们欢呼雀跃，为这一历史性的时刻而庆祝。李昂用自己的行动诠释了"自立为王"的真谛，即依靠自己的力量，建立自己的王国，实现自我治理和独立发展。

5）关键词拼音

- 云隐国：Yún Yǐn Guó
- 勇士：yǒng shì
- 李昂：Lǐ Áng

- 智慧：zhì huì
- 团结：tuán jié
- 军事训练：jūn shì xùn liàn
- 出使：chū shǐ
- 尊重：zūn zhòng
- 庆典：qìng diǎn
- 自立为王：zì lì wéi wáng
- 欢呼雀跃：huān hū què yuè

6）英文故事

In ancient times, there was a remote kingdom called Cloud-Hidden Kingdom, nestled amidst towering mountains and plagued by a scarcity of resources. It was often bullied by neighboring empires, and its aging king was too feeble to govern effectively, leaving the people in dire straits.

Amidst this turmoil, there arose a young warrior named Li Ang. Brave and wise beyond his years, Li Ang harbored a grand ambition: to liberate Cloud-Hidden Kingdom from its misfortunes and establish himself as its king, master of his own destiny.

Understanding that he could not achieve this alone, Li Ang began to rally like-minded individuals, forming a coalition to devise strategies. They strengthened their military, bolstered their nation's strength, and Li Ang himself embarked on diplomatic missions to neighboring kingdoms, earning their respect through his wit and courage, securing a precious window of peace and development for Cloud-Hidden Kingdom.

Years of unwavering effort culminated in a triumphant moment. During a grand celebration, Li Ang formally declared Cloud-Hidden Kingdom's independence, establishing it as a sovereign nation. The people rejoiced, celebrating this historic turning point. Li Ang's journey embodied the essence of "establishing oneself as a king," showcasing the power of self-reliance, governance, and independent development.

Chapter 4: 枉杀无辜

1）成语名称

枉杀无辜

2）成语的拼音

wǎng shā wú gū

3）英文意思

To wrongly execute or harm an innocent person.

4）成语故事（新编）

在古时候的一个小镇上，有一位名叫赵铁的清廉官员。他公正严明，深受百姓爱戴。然而，镇上的恶霸李霸天却对赵铁心怀怨恨，因为赵铁多次阻止了他的不法行为。

一日，李霸天为了报复赵铁，设计了一个阴谋。他暗中收买了一个小偷，让他潜入镇上的富商王家，偷取了一些珍贵的珠宝，并在现场故意留下了一些线索，企图嫁祸给王家的独子王小明。

王小明本是一个善良正直的青年，对珠宝失窃之事一无所知。但由于证据"确凿"，加上李霸天在背后操纵，王小明很快被诬陷为盗贼，并送上了公堂。

赵铁接手了此案，他深知王小明的性格，也察觉到案件中的诸多疑点。然而，在强大的舆论压力和李霸天的暗中阻挠下，赵铁的调查陷入了困境。最终，在一次仓促的审判中，王小明被错判为盗贼，并即将被处以极刑。

就在行刑前一刻，赵铁终于找到了关键的证据，证明了王小明的清白，并揭露了李霸天的阴谋。真相大白后，王小明得以昭雪，而李霸天则受到了应有的惩罚。

赵铁望着王小明被释放的背影，心中充满了愧疚和自责。他深知，如果不是自己的疏忽和外界的压力，王小明本不应遭受这样的冤屈。他暗暗发誓，以后一定要更加谨慎，绝不让任何一个无辜之人枉死在自己手中。

5）关键词拼音

- 赵铁：Zhào Tiě

- 清廉：qīng lián
- 恶霸：è bà
- 李霸天：Lǐ Bà Tiān
- 阴谋：yīn móu
- 嫁祸：jià huò
- 王小明：Wáng Xiǎo Míng
- 善良：shàn liáng
- 证据：zhèng jù
- 冤屈：yuān qū
- 昭雪：zhāo xuě
- 愧疚：kuì jiù
- 自责：zì zé

6）英文故事

In an ancient town, there lived a just and incorruptible official named Zhao Tie, deeply respected by the people. However, the local tyrant Li Batian harbored resentment towards Zhao Tie for his repeated thwarting of his illicit deeds.

One day, Li Batian concocted a plot to avenge himself. He secretly hired a thief to steal valuable jewels from the wealthy merchant Wang's household, deliberately planting clues to frame Wang's only son, Xiao Ming, as the culprit.

Xiao Ming, an innocent and upright youth, had no knowledge of the theft. Yet, due to the seemingly solid evidence and Li Batian's manipulation, Xiao Ming was falsely accused and brought to court.

Zhao Tie, who took on the case, knew Xiao Ming's character and sensed numerous doubts in the matter. Yet, amidst intense public opinion and Li Batian's underhand tactics, Zhao Tie's investigation stalled. In a hasty trial, Xiao Ming was wrongly convicted and sentenced to death.

Just before the execution, Zhao Tie finally uncovered crucial evidence that proved Xiao Ming's innocence and exposed Li Batian's scheme. With the truth revealed, Xiao Ming was exonerated, while Li Batian faced justice.

As Xiao Ming walked free, Zhao Tie was filled with guilt and remorse. He realized that had it not been for his own negligence and external pressures, Xiao Ming would not have suffered such an injustice. He vowed to be more vigilant in the future, ensuring no innocent life was wrongly taken under his watch.

Chapter 5: 金钱非万能

1）成语名称

金钱非万能

2）成语的拼音

jīn qián fēi wàn néng

3）英文意思

Money is not omnipotent.

4）成语故事（新编）

在古老的东方小镇上，有一位名叫李富的商人，他凭借聪明才智和不懈努力积累了巨额财富，成为镇上最富有的人。李富认为金钱是万能的，可以解决一切问题，于是他开始用金钱去购买快乐、尊重和友情。

然而，当他试图用钱来让镇上的孩子们真心地与他玩耍时，却发现他们只是因为他的钱而接近他，一旦没有金钱的诱惑，便疏远了他。当他用金钱去帮助一个陷入困境的朋友时，朋友虽然感激，但心中却总觉得这份帮助带着一丝交易的味道，两人的关系也因此变得微妙。

最终，李富在一次大病中孤独地躺在床上，身边虽有金银财宝无数，却无人真心相伴。这时，他才深刻体会到，虽然金钱能带来物质上的满足，却无法买到真正的情感、理解和陪伴。他意识到，"金钱非万能"，有些东西是金钱永远无法替代的。

5）关键词拼音

- 商人（shāng rén）
- 财富（cái fù）
- 快乐（kuài lè）
- 尊重（zūn zhòng）
- 友情（yǒu qíng）
- 孤独（gū dú）

- 陪伴（péi bàn）
- 深刻（shēn kè）
- 替代（tì dài）

6）英文故事

In an ancient eastern town, there lived a merchant named Li Fu. Through his wisdom and diligence, he amassed a great fortune, becoming the richest man in town. Believing that money was omnipotent, Li Fu began to use it to buy happiness, respect, and friendship.

However, when he tried to buy the sincere companionship of the town's children with money, he found that they only approached him for his wealth, distancing themselves when the lure of money was absent. Similarly, when he offered financial assistance to a friend in distress, the friend, though grateful, felt that the help carried a hint of transaction, subtly altering their relationship.

Eventually, during a severe illness, Li Fu lay alone in bed, surrounded by his vast riches but devoid of genuine companionship. It was then that he profoundly realized that while money could bring material satisfaction, it could never buy true emotions, understanding, or companionship. He came to understand that "Money is not omnipotent," and that there were things money could never replace.

Chapter 6: 登高远眺

1）成语名称

登高远眺

2）成语的拼音

dēng gāo yuǎn tiào

3）英文意思

To ascend to a high place and gaze far into the distance, symbolizing a broad perspective or ambition.

4）成语故事（新编）

古时候，有一位年轻的画家名叫云松，他热衷于描绘壮丽的自然风光。然而，他的画作总显得格局有限，缺乏那种令人心旷神怡的广阔感。一日，云松的师父告诉他："欲得画中山水之神韵，需亲临其境，登高远眺。"

云松听从师父的教诲，背起行囊，踏上了攀登名山的旅程。经过数日艰辛，他终于站在了山顶之上。那一刻，他仿佛置身于天地之间，眼前是连绵不绝的山脉，云雾缭绕，远处的江河如带，城市与田野宛如棋盘般错落有致。云松深深地吸了一口气，心胸豁然开朗，眼前的景象激发了他无尽的创作灵感。

回到画室后，云松的画作发生了翻天覆地的变化，每一幅都充满了磅礴的气势和深远的意境，让人仿佛能随着他的笔触一同遨游于山水之间。他明白了，"登高远眺"不仅让他看到了更广阔的风景，更让他的心灵得到了升华，视野变得更加开阔。

5）关键词拼音

- 画家（huà jiā）
- 师父（shī fu）
- 攀登（pān dēng）
- 山顶（shān dǐng）
- 云雾（yún wù）
- 江河（jiāng hé）

- 创作（chuàng zuò）
- 升华（shēng huá）

6）英文故事

In ancient times, there was a young painter named Yun Song who was passionate about depicting magnificent natural scenery. However, his paintings always seemed limited in scope, lacking the breathtaking sense of vastness. One day, his master told him, "To capture the essence of the mountains and waters in your paintings, you must experience them firsthand by ascending to a high place and gazing far into the distance."

Yun Song followed his master's advice and set out on a journey to climb a famous mountain. After several days of arduous climbing, he finally stood atop the mountain. At that moment, he felt as if he were suspended between heaven and earth, with endless mountains stretching before him, clouds swirling around, and distant rivers appearing like ribbons. Yun Song took a deep breath, and his heart suddenly broadened. The scenery before him inspired him with boundless creative energy.

Upon returning to his studio, Yun Song's paintings underwent a remarkable transformation. Each one was filled with a magnificent momentum and profound artistic conception, allowing viewers to soar through the landscapes with his brushstrokes. He realized that "ascending to a high place and gazing far into the distance" had not only shown him a broader view of the world but also elevated his soul, broadening his horizons.

Chapter 7: 养生送死

1）成语名称

养生送死

2）成语的拼音

yǎng shēng sòng sǐ

3）英文意思

To cultivate health for life and provide proper rites for death, embodying the Chinese concept of respecting both life and death.

4）成语故事（新编）

在古代的一个小镇上，住着一位名叫李老的智者。他一生致力于研究医术与养生之道，不仅自己身体康健，还常常免费为乡亲们治病，深受大家的尊敬。李老深信"养生送死"的道理，认为人活于世，应当珍惜生命，注重保养身体，同时也要为死后做好准备，让生命有一个圆满的结束。

有一次，小镇上的一位老人在临终前，家人因不懂丧葬礼仪而手忙脚乱。李老得知后，亲自前往指导，从为老人擦洗身体、换上寿衣，到安排丧礼的每一个细节，都亲力亲为。他告诉老人的家人："养生，是为了让生命更加美好；送死，则是为了表达对逝者的敬意和怀念。两者缺一不可。"

在李老的帮助下，老人的丧礼办得既庄重又不失温情，让逝者得以安息，也让生者心中得到了慰藉。从此以后，"养生送死"的观念在小镇上深入人心，成为了一种文化传统。

5）关键词拼音

- 智者（zhì zhě）
- 医术（yī shù）
- 养生（yǎng shēng）
- 丧葬礼仪（sāng zàng lǐ yí）
- 寿衣（shòu yī）
- 丧礼（sāng lǐ）

- 敬重（jìng zhòng）
- 文化传统（wén huà chuán tǒng）

6）英文故事

In an ancient town, there lived an wise old man named Li Lao. He devoted his life to studying medicine and the art of preserving health, keeping himself fit and offering free treatment to villagers, earning their profound respect. Li Lao firmly believed in the philosophy of "cultivating health for life and providing proper rites for death," holding that one should cherish life by nurturing one's health and also prepare for death with dignity.

One day, when a senior in the town was on his deathbed, his family was at a loss due to their ignorance of funeral rites. Upon hearing this, Li Lao personally went to guide them, taking care of every detail from washing and dressing the deceased in shrouds to arranging the funeral ceremony. He taught the family, "Cultivating health is to make life more beautiful; providing proper rites for death is to show respect and remembrance to the deceased. Neither is dispensable."

With Li Lao's help, the funeral was solemn yet filled with warmth, allowing the deceased to rest in peace and bringing comfort to the living. From then on, the concept of "cultivating health for life and providing proper rites for death" became deeply rooted in the town's culture, evolving into a cherished tradition.

Chapter 8: 意味深长

1. 成语名称

意味深长

2. 成语的拼音

yì wèi shēn cháng

3. 英文意思

Profound in meaning and significant

4. 成语故事（新编）

在古代的一个小村庄里，有一位智慧的老先生，名叫李墨轩。他虽年事已高，但学识渊博，常常用简短的话语点拨村里的年轻人。有一天，村里的小明因为一次失败而沮丧不已，觉得自己一无是处。李墨轩见状，便邀他至庭院中，指着院中的一棵老梅树说：”你看这梅树，冬日里虽无绿叶繁花，但枝干苍劲，意味深长。它告诉我们，真正的价值不在于一时的繁华，而在于坚韧不拔的精神和深厚的内涵。”小明听后，恍然大悟，明白了失败不过是人生路上的磨砺，而真正的成长在于内心的坚韧与积累。

5. 故事中关键词的拼音

- 智慧（zhì huì）
- 庭院（tíng yuàn）
- 梅树（méi shù）
- 坚韧不拔（jiān rèn bù bá）
- 内涵（nèi hán）
- 磨砺（mó lì）

6. 英文故事

In an ancient village, there lived a wise old man named Li Mohuan. Despite his advanced age, he was knowledgeable and often enlightened the young villagers with concise words. One day, Xiao Ming, a young man in the village, was deeply depressed due to a recent failure, feeling worthless. Observing his plight, Li Mohuan invited him to the courtyard and pointed to an old plum tree, saying, "Look at this plum tree. Though it lacks leaves and blossoms in winter, its branches are vigorous and meaningful, teaching us that true value lies not in momentary splendor but in unyielding spirit and profound depth." Xiao Ming was suddenly enlightened, realizing that failure was merely a trial along life's journey, and true growth came from inner resilience and accumulation.

Chapter 9: 不声不响

1. 成语名称

不声不响

2. 成语的拼音

bù shēng bù xiǎng

3. 英文意思

Without making a sound or fuss; quietly and unobtrusively

4. 成语故事（新编）

在一个宁静的小镇上，住着一位名叫林浩的少年。林浩性格内向，做事总是默默无闻，不声不响。镇上的孩子们都喜欢热闹，经常聚在一起嬉戏打闹，而林浩却总是独自一人在后院里默默练习书法。他的父母起初担心他太过孤僻，但渐渐地，他们发现林浩虽然不声不响，但每一次书法比赛都能带回令人瞩目的奖项。原来，林浩在无人注意的角落里，用汗水和坚持，默默耕耘着自己的梦想。最终，他的才华得到了大家的认可，成为了小镇上人人称赞的少年。

5. 故事中关键词的拼音

- 宁静（níng jìng）
- 内向（nèi xiàng）
- 默默无闻（mò mò wú wén）
- 书法（shū fǎ）
- 耕耘（gēng yún）
- 才华（cái huá）

6. 英文故事

In a peaceful town lived a young boy named Lin Hao. Lin Hao was introverted and always went about his business without making a sound or fuss. While the other children in the town enjoyed noisy gatherings and games, Lin Hao spent his time alone in the backyard, quietly practicing calligraphy. His parents initially worried about his solitude, but gradually they noticed that despite his quiet demeanor, Lin Hao consistently brought home prestigious awards from calligraphy competitions. It turned out that in the corner where no one paid attention, Lin Hao had been silently nurturing his dream with sweat and perseverance. Eventually, his talent was recognized by all, and he became a celebrated youth in the town.

Chapter 10: 多一事不如少一事

1. 成语名称

多一事不如少一事

2. 成语的拼音

duō yī shì bù rú shǎo yī shì

3. 英文意思

Better not to meddle in extra affairs; Less trouble is better than more

4. 成语故事（新编）

在古老的村庄里，住着一位名叫李大爷的智者。他一生秉持着"多一事不如少一事"的原则，生活得平静而和谐。一天，村里两户人家因为一块地界的划分起了争执，双方都各执一词，互不相让，矛盾愈演愈烈。村民们纷纷前来围观，议论纷纷，但谁也不敢轻易插手。这时，李大爷缓缓走来，他先是耐心地听取了双方的意见，然后语重心长地说："乡亲们，俗话说得好，'多一事不如少一事'。大家抬头不见低头见，为了这点小事伤了和气，值得吗？不如各退一步，让出一点地界，既解决了问题，又维护了邻里间的和睦。"在李大爷的劝说下，两家终于握手言和，村民们也纷纷点头赞同，感叹李大爷的智慧与豁达。

5. 故事中关键词的拼音

- 智者（zhì zhě）
- 地界（dì jiè）
- 争执（zhēng zhí）
- 劝说（quàn shuō）
- 握手言和（wò shǒu yán hé）
- 豁达（huò dá）

6. 英文故事

In an ancient village lived an old wise man named Uncle Li. He lived his life by the principle of "better not to meddle in extra affairs." One day, two families in the village fell into a dispute over the division of a piece of land, each side insisting on its own right, and the conflict escalated rapidly. Villagers gathered to watch and discuss, but none dared to interfere. Then Uncle Li walked up slowly. He first listened patiently to both sides and then said sincerely, "My fellow villagers, as the saying goes, 'less trouble is better than more.' We see each other every day; is it worth hurting the harmony for such a trivial matter? Why not each take a step back and give up a little of the land boundary? This will not only solve the problem but also maintain the peace between neighbors." Under Uncle Li's persuasion, the two families finally shook hands and made peace, and the villagers nodded in agreement, marveling at Uncle Li's wisdom and generosity.

Chapter 11: 一步到位

1. 成语名称

一步到位

2. 成语的拼音

yī bù dào wèi

3. 英文意思

Achieve the goal in one step; Accomplish directly and efficiently

4. 成语故事（新编）

在一个充满挑战的项目中，年轻的工程师李明被赋予了设计一座新型桥梁的重任。面对复杂的地理环境、严格的工程要求和紧迫的时间限制，李明没有选择按部就班、分阶段推进的传统方法，而是经过深思熟虑后，决定采用一种创新的设计方案，力求"一步到位"。他夜以继日地工作，反复计算、模拟，最终提出了一套既经济又高效的建桥方案。方案一经提出，便获得了专家组的一致认可，项目因此得以顺利推进，并在预定时间内高质量完成。这座桥梁不仅成为了城市的新地标，也证明了"一步到位"的智慧与力量。

5. 故事中关键词的拼音

- 工程师（gōng chéng shī）
- 挑战（tiǎo zhàn）
- 创新（chuàng xīn）
- 设计（shè jì）
- 高效（gāo xiào）
- 地标（dì biāo）

6. 英文故事

In a challenging project, the young engineer Li Ming was tasked with designing a new type of bridge. Faced with complex geographical conditions, stringent engineering requirements, and tight time constraints, Li Ming chose not to follow the traditional approach of proceeding step by step but instead, after careful consideration, aimed for a "one-step solution." Working tirelessly day and night, he calculated and simulated repeatedly, ultimately proposing an innovative and cost-effective bridge design. Once presented, the plan received unanimous approval from the expert panel, and the project progressed smoothly, completed with high quality within the predetermined timeframe. The bridge not only became a new landmark for the city but also demonstrated the wisdom and power of "achieving the goal in one step."

Chapter 12: 待人诚恳

1. 成语名称

待人诚恳

2. 成语的拼音

dài rén chéng kěn

3. 英文意思

To treat others sincerely and honestly

4. 成语故事（新编）

在一个小村庄里，住着一位名叫王阿姨的妇女。王阿姨以她的善良和诚恳闻名于邻里之间。每当有村民遇到困难，无论是家庭琐事还是农活上的难题，王阿姨总是第一个伸出援手，而且从不求回报。她与人交往时，总是面带微笑，眼神中透露出真诚与关怀，让人感受到温暖和信任。有一次，村里的一位孤寡老人病倒了，王阿姨不仅亲自照顾老人的饮食起居，还四处奔走为老人筹集医药费。她的行为感动了整个村庄，大家纷纷效仿，小村庄因此变得更加和谐友爱。王阿姨用自己的行动诠释了"待人诚恳"的真谛。

5. 故事中关键词的拼音

- 善良（shàn liáng）
- 闻名（wén míng）
- 援手（yuán shǒu）
- 关怀（guān huái）
- 筹集（chóu jí）
- 和谐（hé xié）

6. 英文故事

In a small village, there lived a woman named Aunt Wang, renowned for her kindness and sincerity towards others. Whenever a villager faced difficulties, be it with household chores or agricultural tasks, Aunt Wang was always the first to lend a helping hand, never expecting anything in return. She interacted with people with a warm smile and genuine concern in her eyes, instilling a sense of warmth and trust. Once, when an elderly widow fell ill, Aunt Wang not only personally took care of her daily needs but also went around seeking medical funds. Her actions deeply moved the entire village, inspiring everyone to follow suit, and the small village became more harmonious and loving as a result. Aunt Wang embodied the essence of "treating others sincerely and honestly" through her own deeds.

Chapter 13: 同性相斥

1）成语名称

同性相斥

2）成语的拼音

tóng xìng xiāng chì

3）英文意思

An idiom expressing the idea that similar or like-minded individuals or forces tend to repel or conflict with each other.

4）成语故事（新编）

在古老的智慧之林里，住着两种神奇的生物——光灵与影兽。光灵以阳光为食，散发着温暖与光明；而影兽则隐匿于暗夜，依赖月华生存，带有神秘与幽邃的气息。两者虽同处一片森林，却因本质的不同而鲜有交集。

一日，森林中举办了一场盛大的庆典，邀请所有生灵参与。光灵与影兽在好奇心的驱使下，都不约而同地出席了。然而，当它们相遇时，并未如预期般相互吸引，反而产生了莫名的排斥感。光灵的光芒让影兽感到刺眼，想要逃离；而影兽的幽暗又让光灵觉得压抑，不愿靠近。它们意识到，原来"同性相斥"的法则不仅适用于人与人之间，也存在于这看似截然不同的生命体之间。

从此，光灵与影兽学会了在庆典上保持适当的距离，各自欣赏对方的美丽与独特，而不再试图强行融合。它们明白了，不同的存在有其独特的价值与意义，相互尊重与理解，才是和谐共处的关键。

5）关键词拼音

- 光灵 (guāng líng)
- 影兽 (yǐng shòu)
- 庆典 (qìng diàn)
- 排斥 (pái chì)
- 独特 (dú tè)
- 尊重 (zūn zhòng)

- 和谐 (hé xié)

6）英文故事

In the ancient Wisdom Forest, two mysterious creatures dwelled—the Light Spirits and Shadow Beasts. The Light Spirits fed on sunshine, emitting warmth and light, while the Shadow Beasts hid in the darkness, nourished by moonlight, carrying an aura of mystery and depth. Though sharing the same forest, they rarely interacted due to their inherent differences.

One day, the forest held a grand celebration, inviting all creatures. Out of curiosity, both the Light Spirits and Shadow Beasts attended. But when they met, instead of attracting each other, they felt an inexplicable repulsion. The brightness of the Light Spirits pained the eyes of the Shadow Beasts, driving them away, while the darkness of the Shadow Beasts oppressed the Light Spirits, causing them to shy from them. They realized that the principle of "like attracts like, but similar repels" applied not just to humans but also to these seemingly disparate beings.

From then on, the Light Spirits and Shadow Beasts learned to maintain a respectful distance during celebrations, each appreciating the other's beauty and uniqueness without forcing a union. They understood that different existences hold their own value and significance, and that mutual respect and understanding were the keys to harmonious coexistence.

Chapter 14: 咄咄逼人

1）成语名称

咄咄逼人

2）成语的拼音

duō duō bī rén

3）英文意思

An idiom that describes someone's behavior or words as being extremely aggressive, pushing, or overwhelming to the point of making others feel uncomfortable or intimidated.

4）成语故事（新编）

在古代的一个小镇上，有一位名叫李严的学者，他才华横溢，学识渊博，但性格极为自负。每当与人辩论或交流时，他总是言辞犀利，观点强硬，不给对方丝毫喘息之机。他的气势之盛，仿佛能穿透人心，让人心生畏惧。

一日，镇上举办了一场文学盛会，邀请了众多文人墨客前来交流切磋。李严自然也在受邀之列，他带着满腹经纶，准备大展身手。然而，在会上，每当有人提出不同意见，李严便立刻以他那咄咄逼人的姿态反驳，言辞间充满了不容置疑的权威感。起初，人们还试图与他理性讨论，但很快便被他那强大的气势压得喘不过气来，纷纷选择沉默或退避三舍。

最终，这场文学盛会因李严的咄咄逼人变得气氛凝重，失去了原本应有的轻松与和谐。人们开始意识到，真正的学问与智慧，并不在于如何压倒他人，而在于如何以谦逊之心，倾听不同的声音，共同探索真理的奥秘。

5）关键词拼音

- 李严 (lǐ yán)
- 自负 (zì fù)
- 犀利 (xī lì)
- 气势 (qì shì)
- 权威 (quán wēi)

- 凝重 (níng zhòng)
- 谦逊 (qiān xùn)

6）英文故事

In an ancient town, there lived a scholar named Li Yan, who was brilliant and knowledgeable but overly conceited. Whenever he engaged in debates or conversations, his words were sharp and his stance unyielding, leaving no room for the other person to breathe. His overwhelming presence seemed to pierce through hearts, making others feel intimidated.

One day, the town hosted a grand literary gathering, inviting numerous scholars and poets to exchange ideas. Li Yan, armed with his profound knowledge, was ready to shine. However, as soon as someone presented a differing opinion, Li Yan responded with an aggressive and intimidating demeanor, his every word exuding an air of unquestionable authority. Initially, people tried to engage him in rational discussions, but soon they were overwhelmed by his formidable presence, choosing either to remain silent or retreat.

In the end, the literary gathering turned somber due to Li Yan's aggressive behavior, losing the original ease and harmony. People began to realize that true scholarship and wisdom did not lie in 压倒他人 (压倒他人: yā dǎo tā rén,压倒: overwhelm), but in the humble heart that listens to diverse voices and jointly explores the mysteries of truth.

Chapter 15: 树欲静而风不止

1）成语名称

树欲静而风不止

2）成语的拼音

shù yù jìng ér fēng bù zhǐ

3）英文意思

The tree wants to be still, but the wind won't stop blowing. Metaphorically, it means that one wishes for tranquility but external circumstances or forces prevent it.

4）成语故事（新编）

在一个宁静的山谷里，有一棵古老的松树，它历经风霜，根深叶茂，渴望在岁月的长河中寻得一份宁静与安详。每当夕阳西下，它便轻轻摇曳着枝叶，仿佛在低语："树欲静而风不止。"

一日，山谷外突然刮起了一场前所未有的大风，风势之猛，连山谷中的巨石都被吹得滚动起来。松树虽努力扎根，枝叶却仍被风卷得四散飞舞，无法保持往日的宁静。它心中感叹："我本欲在这山谷中静享岁月，奈何外界的风雨总是不期而至。"

5）关键词拼音

- 山谷 (shān gǔ)
- 松树 (sōng shù)
- 宁静 (níng jìng)
- 夕阳西下 (xī yáng xī xià)
- 摇曳 (yáo yè)
- 枝叶 (zhī yè)
- 风势 (fēng shì)
- 巨石 (jù shí)

- 滚动 (gǔn dòng)
- 风雨 (fēng yǔ)

6）英文故事

In a serene valley, there stood an ancient pine tree, its roots deep and branches lush. It longed for tranquility and peace amidst the passage of time, gently swaying its leaves as the sun set, whispering, "The tree wants to be still, but the wind won't stop blowing."

One day, an unprecedented gale swept in from beyond the valley, its fury so great that even the boulders in the valley were set in motion. Despite the pine's efforts to anchor itself, its branches were whipped about uncontrollably by the wind, unable to maintain its usual serenity. It lamented within, "I had hoped to enjoy the tranquility of this valley, yet the storms of the outside world arrive unexpectedly."

Chapter 16: 火中取栗

1）成语名称

火中取栗

2）成语的拼音

huǒ zhōng qǔ lì

3）英文意思

To pluck chestnuts from the fire; figuratively, to take risks and do someone else's work for little or no reward, often while that person benefits the most.

4）成语故事（新编）

从前，在一个遥远的村庄里，有一只聪明的猴子和一只狡猾的狐狸。秋天，村庄附近的山上长满了成熟的栗子树，但栗子都被烧过的灰烬覆盖着，难以直接取得。狐狸对猴子说："嘿，猴子兄弟，你身手敏捷，不如你去火堆里帮我把栗子捡出来吧，我们平分。"猴子想了想，虽然知道这样做很危险，但还是答应了。它小心翼翼地接近火堆，用尾巴扇风降低火势，最终成功地取出了一些栗子。然而，当猴子满心欢喜地回来准备与狐狸分享时，却发现狐狸早已带着栗子逃之夭夭，留下猴子独自面对可能还未完全熄灭的火堆。

5）关键词拼音

- 猴子 (hóu zi)
- 狐狸 (hú li)
- 栗子 (lì zi)
- 火堆 (huǒ duī)
- 身手敏捷 (shēn shǒu mǐn jié)
- 小心翼翼 (xiǎo xīn yì yì)
- 灰烬 (huī jìn)
- 逃之夭夭 (táo zhī yāo yāo)

6）英文故事

Once upon a time, in a faraway village, there lived a clever monkey and a cunning fox. In autumn, the mountains surrounding the village were filled with ripe chestnut trees, but the nuts were buried beneath layers of ash from a recent fire, making them difficult to reach. The fox approached the monkey, saying, "Hey, Monkey brother, with your agility, why don't you retrieve the chestnuts from the fire for me? We'll split them evenly." The monkey, though knowing the danger, agreed. It cautiously approached the fire, using its tail to fan away the flames, and finally managed to retrieve some chestnuts. But when the monkey happily returned to share with the fox, it found that the fox had already fled with the nuts, leaving the monkey alone, facing the potentially still-smoldering fire.

Chapter 17: 功夫不负有心人

1）成语名称

功夫不负有心人

2）成语的拼音

gōng fū bù fù yǒu xīn rén

3）英文意思

Efforts will eventually be rewarded; diligence pays off in the end.

4）成语故事（新编）

在古时候，有一个名叫李明的书生，他自幼家境贫寒，却对学问有着无比的热爱和执着。每天天未亮，李明便已起身，借着微弱的烛光苦读诗书，夜晚则借着月光继续研习，日复一日，年复一年，从未有过懈怠。乡亲们都笑他傻，认为读书无用，但李明坚信"功夫不负有心人"。

终于，在一次科举考试中，李明凭借着深厚的学识和不懈的努力，一举夺魁，成为了当年的状元。消息传回村里，那些曾经嘲笑他的人无不惊叹，纷纷称赞李明的勤奋与毅力。李明用自己的经历证明了，只要坚持不懈地努力，就一定能够取得成功。

5）关键词拼音

- 李明 (lǐ míng)
- 书生 (shū shēng)
- 贫寒 (pín hán)
- 热爱 (rè ài)
- 执着 (zhí zhuó)
- 烛光 (zhú guāng)
- 苦读 (kǔ dú)
- 懈怠 (xiè dài)
- 科举考试 (kē jǔ kǎo shì)

- 状元 (zhuàng yuán)

6）英文故事

In ancient times, there was a scholar named Li Ming who, despite coming from a poor family, had an insatiable love and perseverance for learning. Every day, before dawn, Li Ming would rise and diligently study under the dim light of a candle, continuing his studies by moonlight into the night, never slacking off. The villagers mocked him, believing that studying was futile, but Li Ming firmly believed that "efforts will eventually be rewarded."

Eventually, during the imperial examination, Li Ming, with his profound knowledge and relentless dedication, emerged victorious as the top scholar of the year, the Zhuangyuan. News of his achievement spread back to the village, astonishing those who had once ridiculed him and earning their praise for his diligence and perseverance. Li Ming's story became a testament that with unwavering effort, one can indeed achieve success.

Chapter 18: 载歌载舞

1）成语名称

载歌载舞

2）成语的拼音

zài gē zài wǔ

3）英文意思

To sing and dance joyfully; expressing great happiness or celebration.

4）成语故事（新编）

在一个风和日丽的春日里，小村庄迎来了一年一度的丰收节。村民们为了庆祝这一年的辛勤耕耘终于换来了满仓的粮食，决定举办一场盛大的庆祝活动。清晨，随着第一缕阳光洒满大地，村民们便开始忙碌起来，布置会场、准备美食。到了傍晚，整个村庄张灯结彩，热闹非凡。

随着一阵欢快的锣鼓声响起，庆祝活动正式拉开序幕。村民们纷纷走上舞台，有的拿起手鼓，有的挥舞彩绸，还有的则手拉手围成圈，开始了载歌载舞的表演。歌声悠扬，舞姿翩跹，每一个动作都充满了对生活的热爱和对未来的憧憬。孩子们在人群中穿梭嬉戏，笑声与歌声交织在一起，整个村庄沉浸在一片欢乐祥和的氛围之中。

5）关键词拼音

- 丰收节 (fēng shōu jié)
- 辛勤耕耘 (xīn qín gēng yún)
- 锣鼓声 (luó gǔ shēng)
- 布置会场 (bù zhì huì chǎng)
- 美食 (měi shí)
- 张灯结彩 (zhāng dēng jié cǎi)
- 热闹非凡 (rè nào fēi fán)
- 舞姿翩跹 (wǔ zī piān xiān)
- 憧憬 (chōng jǐng)

- 祥和 (xiáng hé)

6）英文故事

On a sunny spring day, the small village celebrated its annual Harvest Festival. To mark the fruitful year of hard work that had yielded full barns of grain, the villagers organized a grand celebration. From early morning, as the first rays of sunlight illuminated the land, they bustled about, decorating the venue and preparing delicious dishes. By evening, the entire village was adorned with lanterns and colored streamers, buzzing with excitement.

With the resounding beat of drums and gongs, the festivities commenced. The villagers took to the stage, some brandishing hand drums, others waving colorful silks, and still others forming circles, engaging in a joyous display of singing and dancing. The melodies soared, the dances graceful, each movement imbued with love for life and visions for the future. Children darted between the adults, their laughter mingling with the songs, enveloping the entire village in a warm and harmonious atmosphere of joy.

Chapter 19: 排忧解难

1）成语名称

排忧解难

2）成语的拼音

pái yōu jiě nàn

3）英文意思

To alleviate worries and resolve difficulties; to provide assistance in times of trouble.

4）成语故事（新编）

在古老的村庄里，住着一位智慧而仁慈的老者，名叫李伯。李伯不仅精通农耕之术，更擅长为人排忧解难。每当村中有人遇到难题或心中忧愁，都会找李伯倾诉。

有一年，村庄遭遇了前所未有的干旱，庄稼枯萎，水源枯竭，村民们忧心忡忡，生活陷入困境。村长带领大家尝试了各种方法，但都无济于事。绝望之中，大家想到了李伯，纷纷前往求教。

李伯听闻后，没有立即给出答案，而是带着几位年轻人翻山越岭，寻找新的水源。经过数日的艰难探索，他们终于在一处隐蔽的山谷中发现了一股清泉。李伯又组织村民修建水渠，将清泉引入村庄，解决了灌溉和生活用水的问题。

同时，李伯还教村民们如何种植耐旱作物，调整种植结构，以应对未来的干旱。在他的帮助下，村庄逐渐恢复了往日的生机与活力，村民们心中的忧愁也随之消散。从此，李伯被尊称为"排忧解难"的智者，他的故事也在村中流传开来，激励着后人面对困难时要勇于寻求解决之道。

5）关键词拼音

- 村庄 (cūn zhuāng)
- 智者 (zhì zhě)
- 干旱 (gān hàn)
- 忧愁 (yōu chóu)

- 水源 (shuǐ yuán)
- 翻山越岭 (fān shān yuè lǐng)
- 清泉 (qīng quán)
- 水渠 (shuǐ qú)
- 耐旱作物 (nài hàn zuò wù)
- 激励 (jī lì)

6）英文故事

In an ancient village, there lived an elderly man named Uncle Li, who was both wise and kind-hearted. Uncle Li was renowned for his ability to alleviate worries and resolve difficulties for the villagers. Whenever someone encountered a problem or was weighed down by sorrow, they would turn to Uncle Li for advice.

One year, the village was struck by an unprecedented drought, with crops wilting and water sources drying up, plunging the villagers into despair. The village head led efforts to find solutions, but to no avail. In desperation, they sought Uncle Li's wisdom.

Upon hearing their plight, Uncle Li didn't immediately offer a solution but instead led a group of young men on a trek through mountains and valleys in search of new water sources. After several days of arduous exploration, they discovered a hidden spring in a secluded valley. Uncle Li then organized the villagers to construct an aqueduct, channeling the clear spring water into the village, resolving the irrigation and drinking water crisis.

Furthermore, Uncle Li taught the villagers how to cultivate drought-resistant crops and adjust their farming practices to withstand future droughts. With his guidance, the village gradually regained its vitality, and the villagers' worries dissipated. From then on, Uncle Li was hailed as the "wise man who dispels worries and resolves difficulties," and his story became a legend in the village, inspiring future generations to face challenges with courage and ingenuity.

Chapter 20: 摩肩接踵

1）成语名称

摩肩接踵

2）成语的拼音

mó jiān jiē zhǒng

3）英文意思

Shoulders rubbing and heels touching; extremely crowded.

4）成语故事（新编）

在古代的一个繁华都市中，每年春节都会举办盛大的庙会。这一年，庙会格外热闹，吸引了四面八方的百姓前来参与。街道上，商贩们摆满了各式各样的摊位，叫卖声此起彼伏；小吃摊前，香气四溢，引得人们纷纷驻足品尝。

随着夜幕降临，花灯初上，庙会达到了高潮。人们穿着节日的盛装，手提灯笼，结伴而行。由于人流量实在太大，人群开始变得异常拥挤，几乎每个人都在不由自主地"摩肩接踵"——肩膀与肩膀紧紧相贴，脚跟与脚跟几乎相连，前行都变得异常艰难。但即便如此，大家的脸上都洋溢着节日的喜悦，享受着这份难得的热闹与团聚。

5）关键词拼音

- 庙会 (miào huì)
- 繁华 (fán huá)
- 商贩 (shāng fàn)
- 摊位 (tān wèi)
- 拥挤 (yōng jǐ)
- 盛装 (shèng zhuāng)
- 灯笼 (dēng long)
- 团聚 (tuán jù)
- 喜悦 (xǐ yuè)

6）英文故事

In an ancient bustling metropolis, the annual Spring Festival temple fair was held with unprecedented grandeur. This year, the fair attracted people from all corners of the land, eager to participate in the festivities. The streets were lined with various stalls, where merchants' cries for sales echoed through the air, while snack booths exuded mouth-watering aromas, drawing crowds to indulge in the culinary delights.

As night fell and lanterns illuminated the scene, the temple fair reached its climax. People, dressed in festive attire and carrying lanterns, walked in groups, their faces beaming with joy. However, the sheer volume of people made the crowds exceedingly dense, with individuals finding themselves in a state of "mó jiān jiē zhǒng" – shoulders rubbing against shoulders and heels almost touching, making it difficult to move forward. Yet, despite the congestion, everyone was immersed in the festive atmosphere, cherishing the rare moments of excitement and reunion.

Milton Keynes UK
Ingram Content Group UK Ltd.
UKHW030807220724
445981UK00011B/463